SIMPLY
GIVE THANKS
Gratitude Journal

MELISSA ALVAREZ

Adrema Press

Author Websites: www.MelissaAlvarez.com and www.APsychicHaven.com

ISBN: 978-1-59611-111-0

Cover and Book Design by Melissa Alvarez at BookCovers.Us
Cover Art Background © DepositPhotos.com / David Schrader / Konstanttin

First Trade Paperback Printing: June 2013
10 9 8 7 6 5 4 3 2 1

Other books by Melissa Alvarez

365 Ways to Raise Your Frequency
The 365 Days to Raise Your Frequency Journal
Your Psychic Self
Simply Give Thanks
Simply Give Thanks Gratitude Journal
Analyze Your Handwriting
Your Color Power
Ghosts, A Spirit Guide and A Past Life
Chakra Divination® Cards & Charts Activity Book
The Essential Guide To Chakra Divination
Chakra Divination Ultimate Balance Journal
The eLink Directory of Paranormal Investigative Groups Around the World
Homemade Recipes for Horse Treats plus Fly Sprays & Tips for Owners
The Phoenix's Guide To Self Renewal
Christmas Desserts
Penelope Panda's Shooting Star

Writing as Ariana Dupré
Paranormal Romantic Suspense

Night Visions
Paradise Designs
Briar Mountain
Talgorian Dragon
Talgorian Prophecy

Websites:
MelissaA.com
BookCoversGalore.com
BookCovers.Us
APsychicHaven.com

Date: ______________

Today I'm grateful for: ______________

My Thoughts about the Day: ______________

Date: ________________

Today I'm grateful for: ____________________________________

My Thoughts about the Day: ______________________________

Date: ________________

Today I'm grateful for: ____________________________________

My Thoughts about the Day: ______________________________

Date: ________________

Today I'm grateful for: ____________________________________

My Thoughts about the Day: ____________________________

Date: ____________

Today I'm grateful for: ______________________________

My Thoughts about the Day: ______________________________

Date: ________________

Today I'm grateful for: ____________________________________

My Thoughts about the Day: ______________________________

Date: ______________

Today I'm grateful for: ______________________________

My Thoughts about the Day: ______________________________

Date: ________________

Today I'm grateful for: ____________________________________

My Thoughts about the Day: ____________________________

Date: ________________

Today I'm grateful for: ____________________________________

My Thoughts about the Day: ______________________________

Date: ________________

Today I'm grateful for: ________________

My Thoughts about the Day: ________________

Date: ________________

Today I'm grateful for: ____________________________________

My Thoughts about the Day: ____________________________

Date: ________________

Today I'm grateful for: ________________

My Thoughts about the Day: ________________

Date: ________________

Today I'm grateful for: ___________________________________

My Thoughts about the Day: ______________________________

Date: ______________

Today I'm grateful for: ______________

My Thoughts about the Day: ______________

Date: ________________

Today I'm grateful for: ________________

My Thoughts about the Day: ________________

Date: ______________

Today I'm grateful for: ______________

My Thoughts about the Day: ______________

Date: ________________

Today I'm grateful for:

My Thoughts about the Day:

Date: ______________

Today I'm grateful for: ______________

My Thoughts about the Day: ______________

Date: ______________

Today I'm grateful for: ______________

My Thoughts about the Day: ______________

Date: ____________

Today I'm grateful for: ____________

My Thoughts about the Day: ____________

Date: ____________________

Today I'm grateful for: ____

My Thoughts about the Day: ________________________________

Date: ______________

Today I'm grateful for: ______________

My Thoughts about the Day: ______________

Date: ________________

Today I'm grateful for: ______________________________

My Thoughts about the Day: ________________________

Date: ________________

Today I'm grateful for: ____________________________________

My Thoughts about the Day: ______________________________

Date: ________________

Today I'm grateful for: ________________

My Thoughts about the Day: ________________

Date: ________________

Today I'm grateful for: ____________________________________

My Thoughts about the Day: ______________________________

Date: ________________

Today I'm grateful for: ___________________________________

My Thoughts about the Day: ___________________________

Date: ________________

Today I'm grateful for: ____________________________________

My Thoughts about the Day: ______________________________

Date: ________________

Today I'm grateful for: ______________________________

My Thoughts about the Day: ______________________________

Date: ______________

Today I'm grateful for: ______________________________

My Thoughts about the Day: ______________________________

Date: ________________

Today I'm grateful for: ________________

My Thoughts about the Day: ________________

Date: ________________

Today I'm grateful for: ________________

My Thoughts about the Day: ________________

Date: ________________

Today I'm grateful for: ________________

My Thoughts about the Day: ________________

Date: ______________

Today I'm grateful for: ______________

My Thoughts about the Day: ______________

Date: ________________

Today I'm grateful for: ________________

My Thoughts about the Day: ________________

Date: ________________

Today I'm grateful for: ____________________________________

My Thoughts about the Day: ______________________________

Date: ________________

Today I'm grateful for: ________________

My Thoughts about the Day: ________________

Date: ________________

Today I'm grateful for: ________________

My Thoughts about the Day: ________________

Date: ______________

Today I'm grateful for: ______________

My Thoughts about the Day: ______________

Date: ______________

Today I'm grateful for: ______________________________

My Thoughts about the Day: ______________________________

Date: ______________

Today I'm grateful for: ______________

My Thoughts about the Day: ______________

Date: ________________

Today I'm grateful for: ________________________________

My Thoughts about the Day: ________________________________

Date: ______________

Today I'm grateful for: ______________

My Thoughts about the Day: ______________

Date: ________________

Today I'm grateful for: ________________________________

My Thoughts about the Day: ________________________________

Date: ________________

Today I'm grateful for: ________________

My Thoughts about the Day: ________________

Date: ________________

Today I'm grateful for: ________________

My Thoughts about the Day: ________________

Date: ________________

Today I'm grateful for: ________________

My Thoughts about the Day: ________________

Date: ________________

Today I'm grateful for: ____________________________________

My Thoughts about the Day: ______________________________

Date: ________________

Today I'm grateful for: ____________________________________

My Thoughts about the Day: ____________________________________

Date: ________________

Today I'm grateful for: ________________

My Thoughts about the Day: ________________

Date: ________________

Today I'm grateful for: ________________

My Thoughts about the Day: ________________

Date: ________________

Today I'm grateful for: ____________________________________

My Thoughts about the Day: ______________________________

Date: ________________

Today I'm grateful for: ____________________________________

My Thoughts about the Day: ______________________________

Date: ________________

Today I'm grateful for: ________________

My Thoughts about the Day: ________________

Date: ________________

Today I'm grateful for: ____________________________________

My Thoughts about the Day: ______________________________

Date: ________________

Today I'm grateful for: ________________________________

My Thoughts about the Day: ____________________________

Date: ____________

Today I'm grateful for: ____________

My Thoughts about the Day: ____________

Date: ________________

Today I'm grateful for: ________________

My Thoughts about the Day: ________________

Date: ____________________

Today I'm grateful for: ____________________

My Thoughts about the Day: ____________________

Date: ________________

Today I'm grateful for: ________________

My Thoughts about the Day: ________________

Date: ________________

Today I'm grateful for: ______________________________________

My Thoughts about the Day: ______________________________

Date: ________________

Today I'm grateful for: ____________________________________

My Thoughts about the Day: ______________________________

Date: ______________

Today I'm grateful for: ______________

My Thoughts about the Day: ______________

Date: ________________

Today I'm grateful for: ________________________________

My Thoughts about the Day: ______________________________

Date: ______________

Today I'm grateful for: ____

My Thoughts about the Day: ____________________________________

Date: ________________

Today I'm grateful for: ____________________________________

My Thoughts about the Day: ______________________________

Date: ________________

Today I'm grateful for: ________________

My Thoughts about the Day: ________________

Date: ________________

Today I'm grateful for: ____________________________________

My Thoughts about the Day: ______________________________

Date: ________________

Today I'm grateful for: ____________________________________

My Thoughts about the Day: ______________________________

Date: ________________

Today I'm grateful for: ____________________________________

My Thoughts about the Day: ______________________________

Date: ________________

Today I'm grateful for: ________________

My Thoughts about the Day: ________________

Date: ________________

Today I'm grateful for: ________________

My Thoughts about the Day: ________________

Date: ____________

Today I'm grateful for: ____________

My Thoughts about the Day: ____________

Date: ________________

Today I'm grateful for: ________________________________

My Thoughts about the Day: ____________________________

Date: ________________

Today I'm grateful for: ________________

My Thoughts about the Day: ________________

Date: ________________

Today I'm grateful for: ____________________________________

My Thoughts about the Day: ______________________________

Date: ______________

Today I'm grateful for: ______________________________

My Thoughts about the Day: ______________________________

Date: ______________

Today I'm grateful for: ______________

My Thoughts about the Day: ______________

Date: ________________

Today I'm grateful for: ____________________________________

My Thoughts about the Day: ______________________________

Date: ____________________

Today I'm grateful for: ____________________

My Thoughts about the Day: ____________________

Date: ________________

Today I'm grateful for: ______________________________

My Thoughts about the Day: ______________________________

Date: ______________

Today I'm grateful for: ______________

My Thoughts about the Day: ______________

Date: ________________

Today I'm grateful for: ________________

My Thoughts about the Day: ________________

Date: ________________

Today I'm grateful for: ____________________

My Thoughts about the Day: ____________________

Date: ______________

Today I'm grateful for: ______________

My Thoughts about the Day: ______________

Date: ______________

Today I'm grateful for: ______________________________

My Thoughts about the Day: ______________________________

Date: ______________

Today I'm grateful for: ______________

My Thoughts about the Day: ______________

Date: ______________

Today I'm grateful for: ______________________________

My Thoughts about the Day: ______________________________

Date: ___________________

Today I'm grateful for: ___________________

My Thoughts about the Day: ___________________

Date: ________________

Today I'm grateful for: ________________________

My Thoughts about the Day: ________________________

Date: ____________

Today I'm grateful for: ____________

My Thoughts about the Day: ____________

Date: ___

Today I'm grateful for: ___

My Thoughts about the Day: ___

Date: ________________

Today I'm grateful for: ________________

My Thoughts about the Day: ________________

Date: ________________

Today I'm grateful for: ______________________________

My Thoughts about the Day: __________________________

Date: ________________

Today I'm grateful for: ____________________________________

My Thoughts about the Day: ____________________________

Date: ______________

Today I'm grateful for: ______________

My Thoughts about the Day: ______________

Date: ____________

Today I'm grateful for: ______________________________

My Thoughts about the Day: ______________________________

Date: ________________

Today I'm grateful for: ___________________________________

My Thoughts about the Day: ______________________________

Date: ________________

Today I'm grateful for: ________________

My Thoughts about the Day: ________________

Date: ________________

Today I'm grateful for: ____________________________________

My Thoughts about the Day: ______________________________

Date: ________________

Today I'm grateful for: ____________________________________

My Thoughts about the Day: ______________________________

Date: ____________________

Today I'm grateful for: ____________________

My Thoughts about the Day: ____________________

Date: ________________

Today I'm grateful for: ________________

My Thoughts about the Day: ________________

Date: ______________

Today I'm grateful for: ______________________________

My Thoughts about the Day: ______________________________

Date: ______________

Today I'm grateful for: ______________

My Thoughts about the Day: ______________

Date: ________________

Today I'm grateful for: ________________________________

My Thoughts about the Day: ________________________________

Date: ____________

Today I'm grateful for: ____________

My Thoughts about the Day: ____________

Date: ________________

Today I'm grateful for: ____________________________________

My Thoughts about the Day: ______________________________

Date: ________________

Today I'm grateful for: ____________________________________

My Thoughts about the Day: ______________________________

Date: ________________

Today I'm grateful for: ________________

My Thoughts about the Day: ________________

Date: ______________

Today I'm grateful for: ______________

My Thoughts about the Day: ______________

Date: ________________

Today I'm grateful for: ___________________________________

My Thoughts about the Day: ______________________________

Date: ________________

Today I'm grateful for:

My Thoughts about the Day:

Date: ________________

Today I'm grateful for: ____________________________________

My Thoughts about the Day: ______________________________

Date: ________________

Today I'm grateful for: ____________________________________

My Thoughts about the Day: ______________________________

Date: ________________

Today I'm grateful for: ________________

My Thoughts about the Day: ________________

Date: ____________

Today I'm grateful for: ____________

My Thoughts about the Day: ____________

Date: ________________

Today I'm grateful for: ________________________________

My Thoughts about the Day: ________________________________

Date: ________________

Today I'm grateful for: ________________

My Thoughts about the Day: ________________

Date: ________________

Today I'm grateful for: ____________________________________

My Thoughts about the Day: ______________________________

Date: ________________

Today I'm grateful for: ____________________________________

My Thoughts about the Day: ______________________________

Date: ________________

Today I'm grateful for: ____________________________________

My Thoughts about the Day: ____________________________

Date: ________________

Today I'm grateful for: ________________________________

My Thoughts about the Day: ________________________________

Date: ________________

Today I'm grateful for: ____________________________________

My Thoughts about the Day: ____________________________

Date: ________________

Today I'm grateful for: ________________

My Thoughts about the Day: ________________

Date: ________________

Today I'm grateful for: ___________________________________

My Thoughts about the Day: ___________________________

Date: ____________

Today I'm grateful for: ____________

My Thoughts about the Day: ____________

Date: ________________

Today I'm grateful for: ________________

My Thoughts about the Day: ________________

Date: ________________

Today I'm grateful for: ________________

My Thoughts about the Day: ________________

Date: ________________

Today I'm grateful for: ______________________________

My Thoughts about the Day: __________________________

Date: ________________

Today I'm grateful for: ________________________________

My Thoughts about the Day: ____________________________

Date: ________________

Today I'm grateful for: ________________________________

My Thoughts about the Day: ________________________

Date: ________________

Today I'm grateful for: ________________

My Thoughts about the Day: ________________

Date: ________________

Today I'm grateful for: ________________

My Thoughts about the Day: ________________

Date: ________________

Today I'm grateful for: ____________________________________

My Thoughts about the Day: ____________________________________

Date: ________________

Today I'm grateful for: ________________________________

My Thoughts about the Day: ________________________________

Date: ______________

Today I'm grateful for: ______________

My Thoughts about the Day: ______________

Date: ________________

Today I'm grateful for: ____________________________________

My Thoughts about the Day: ______________________________

Date: ________________

Today I'm grateful for: ________________________________

My Thoughts about the Day: ____________________________

Date: ____________________

Today I'm grateful for: ____

My Thoughts about the Day: ____________________________________

Date: ________________

Today I'm grateful for: ________________________________

My Thoughts about the Day: ______________________________

Date: ________________

Today I'm grateful for: ________________

My Thoughts about the Day: ________________

Date: ________________

Today I'm grateful for: ________________

My Thoughts about the Day: ________________

Date: ________________

Today I'm grateful for: ________________

My Thoughts about the Day: ________________

Date: ________________

Today I'm grateful for: ________________

My Thoughts about the Day: ________________

Date: ________________

Today I'm grateful for: ____________________________________

My Thoughts about the Day: ______________________________

Date: ______________

Today I'm grateful for: ______________________________

My Thoughts about the Day: ______________________________

Date: ________________

Today I'm grateful for: ____________________________________

My Thoughts about the Day: ______________________________

Date: ________________

Today I'm grateful for: ____________________________________

My Thoughts about the Day: ______________________________

Date: ____________________

Today I'm grateful for: ____________________

My Thoughts about the Day: ____________________

Date: ________________

Today I'm grateful for: ________________

My Thoughts about the Day: ________________

Date: ________________

Today I'm grateful for: ____________________________________

My Thoughts about the Day: ________________________________

Date: ________________

Today I'm grateful for: ________________

My Thoughts about the Day: ________________

Date: ___________________

Today I'm grateful for: ___________________

My Thoughts about the Day: ___________________

Date: ________________

Today I'm grateful for: ________________

My Thoughts about the Day: ________________

Date: ______________

Today I'm grateful for: ______________

My Thoughts about the Day: ______________

Date: ________________

Today I'm grateful for: ________________________________

My Thoughts about the Day: ________________________________

Date: ________________

Today I'm grateful for: ____________________________________

My Thoughts about the Day: ______________________________

Date: ________________

Today I'm grateful for: ______________________________

My Thoughts about the Day: __________________________

Date: ___________________

Today I'm grateful for: ____

My Thoughts about the Day: ____________________________

Date: ______________

Today I'm grateful for: ______________

My Thoughts about the Day: ______________

Date: ________________

Today I'm grateful for: ____________________________________

My Thoughts about the Day: ______________________________

Date: ________________

Today I'm grateful for: ________________________________

My Thoughts about the Day: ________________________________

Date: ________________

Today I'm grateful for: ___________________________________

My Thoughts about the Day: ______________________________

Date: ________________

Today I'm grateful for: ________________

My Thoughts about the Day: ________________

Date: ________________

Today I'm grateful for: ______________________________________

My Thoughts about the Day: ______________________________

Date: ______________

Today I'm grateful for: ______________________________

My Thoughts about the Day: ______________________________

Date: ________________

Today I'm grateful for: ____________________________________

My Thoughts about the Day: ______________________________

Date: ________________

Today I'm grateful for: ______________________________

My Thoughts about the Day: ______________________________

Date: ______________

Today I'm grateful for: ______________

My Thoughts about the Day: ______________

Date: ______________

Today I'm grateful for: ______________________________

My Thoughts about the Day: ______________________

Date: ______________

Today I'm grateful for: ______________

My Thoughts about the Day: ______________

Date: ________________

Today I'm grateful for: ________________

My Thoughts about the Day: ________________

Date: ______________

Today I'm grateful for: ______________

My Thoughts about the Day: ______________

Date: ________________

Today I'm grateful for: ________________

My Thoughts about the Day: ________________

Date: ________________

Today I'm grateful for: ________________

My Thoughts about the Day: ________________

Date: ______________

Today I'm grateful for: ______________________________

My Thoughts about the Day: ______________________________

Date: ________________

Today I'm grateful for: ______________________________

My Thoughts about the Day: ________________________

Date: ________________

Today I'm grateful for: ________________

My Thoughts about the Day: ________________

Date: ______________

Today I'm grateful for: ______________________________

My Thoughts about the Day: ______________________________

Date: ________________

Today I'm grateful for: ____________________________________

My Thoughts about the Day: ______________________________

Date: ________________

Today I'm grateful for: ____________________________________

My Thoughts about the Day: ______________________________

Date: ________________

Today I'm grateful for: ________________________________

My Thoughts about the Day: ____________________________

Date: ____________

Today I'm grateful for: ____________

My Thoughts about the Day: ____________

Date: ________________

Today I'm grateful for: ________________

My Thoughts about the Day: ________________

Date: ________________

Today I'm grateful for: ____________________________________

My Thoughts about the Day: ______________________________

Date: ________________

Today I'm grateful for: ________________________________

My Thoughts about the Day: ________________________________

Date: ________________

Today I'm grateful for: ____________________________________

My Thoughts about the Day: ________________________________

Date: ______________

Today I'm grateful for: ______________

My Thoughts about the Day: ______________

Date: ________________

Today I'm grateful for: ________________

My Thoughts about the Day: ________________

Date: ________________

Today I'm grateful for: ____________________________________

My Thoughts about the Day: ______________________________

Date: ________________

Today I'm grateful for: ____________________________________

My Thoughts about the Day: ____________________________

Date: ______________

Today I'm grateful for: ______________

My Thoughts about the Day: ______________

Date: ________________

Today I'm grateful for: ____________________________________

My Thoughts about the Day: ______________________________

Date: ________________

Today I'm grateful for: ____________________________________

My Thoughts about the Day: ____________________________________

Date: ________________

Today I'm grateful for: ________________

My Thoughts about the Day: ________________

Date: ________________

Today I'm grateful for: ____________________________________

My Thoughts about the Day: ______________________________

Date: ________________

Today I'm grateful for: __________________________________

My Thoughts about the Day: ____________________________

Date: ________________

Today I'm grateful for: ________________________________

My Thoughts about the Day: ________________________________

Date: ________________

Today I'm grateful for: ____________________________________

My Thoughts about the Day: ____________________________

Date: ____________

Today I'm grateful for: ____________

My Thoughts about the Day: ____________

Date: ____________________

Today I'm grateful for: ____________________

My Thoughts about the Day: ____________________

Date: ________________

Today I'm grateful for: ________________________________

My Thoughts about the Day: ______________________________

Date: ________________

Today I'm grateful for: ____________________________________

My Thoughts about the Day: ______________________________

Date: ________________

Today I'm grateful for: ________________________________

My Thoughts about the Day: ________________________________

Date: ________________

Today I'm grateful for: ____________________________________

My Thoughts about the Day: ______________________________

Date: ________________

Today I'm grateful for: ________________________________

My Thoughts about the Day: ____________________________

Date: ________________

Today I'm grateful for: ________________

My Thoughts about the Day: ________________

Date: ________________

Today I'm grateful for: ______________________________

My Thoughts about the Day: __________________________

Date: ________________

Today I'm grateful for: ________________

My Thoughts about the Day: ________________

Date: ___

Today I'm grateful for: ___

My Thoughts about the Day: ___

Date: ________________

Today I'm grateful for: ________________

My Thoughts about the Day: ________________

Date: ________________

Today I'm grateful for: ____________________________________

My Thoughts about the Day: ____________________________

Date: ________________

Today I'm grateful for: ____________________________________

My Thoughts about the Day: ______________________________

Date: ________________

Today I'm grateful for: ________________________________

My Thoughts about the Day: ________________________________

Date: ________________

Today I'm grateful for: ____________________________________

My Thoughts about the Day: ______________________________

Date: ________________

Today I'm grateful for: ________________

My Thoughts about the Day: ________________

Date: ________________

Today I'm grateful for: ____________________________________

My Thoughts about the Day: ______________________________

Date: ________________

Today I'm grateful for: ____________________________________

My Thoughts about the Day: ______________________________

Date: ______________

Today I'm grateful for: ______________

My Thoughts about the Day: ______________

Date: ________________

Today I'm grateful for: ____________________________________

My Thoughts about the Day: ______________________________

Date: ________________

Today I'm grateful for: ___________________________________

My Thoughts about the Day: ______________________________

Date: ________________

Today I'm grateful for: ___________________________________

My Thoughts about the Day: ______________________________

Date: ________________

Today I'm grateful for: ______________________________

My Thoughts about the Day: __________________________

Date: ________________

Today I'm grateful for: ________________

My Thoughts about the Day: ________________

Date: ________________

Today I'm grateful for: ___________________________________

My Thoughts about the Day: ______________________________

Date: ________________

Today I'm grateful for: ______________________________

My Thoughts about the Day: ________________________

Date: ________________

Today I'm grateful for: ___________________________________

My Thoughts about the Day: ______________________________

Date: ______________

Today I'm grateful for: ______________________________

My Thoughts about the Day: ______________________________

Date: ________________

Today I'm grateful for: ______________________________

My Thoughts about the Day: __________________________

Date: ________________

Today I'm grateful for: ____________________________________

My Thoughts about the Day: ______________________________

Date: ________________

Today I'm grateful for: ________________

My Thoughts about the Day: ________________

Date: ________________

Today I'm grateful for: ______________________________

My Thoughts about the Day: ______________________________

Date: ________________

Today I'm grateful for: ________________

My Thoughts about the Day: ________________

Date: ______________

Today I'm grateful for: ______________________________

My Thoughts about the Day: ______________________________

Date: ________________

Today I'm grateful for: ____________________________________

My Thoughts about the Day: ______________________________

Date: ________________

Today I'm grateful for: ____________________________________

My Thoughts about the Day: ____________________________

Date: ________________

Today I'm grateful for: ____________________________________

My Thoughts about the Day: ______________________________

Date: ________________

Today I'm grateful for: ________________

My Thoughts about the Day: ________________

Date: ________________

Today I'm grateful for: ______________________________

My Thoughts about the Day: __________________________

Date: ________________

Today I'm grateful for: ____________________________________

My Thoughts about the Day: ______________________________

Date: ________________

Today I'm grateful for: ________________

My Thoughts about the Day: ________________

Date: ________________

Today I'm grateful for: ____________________________________

My Thoughts about the Day: ______________________________

Date: ________________

Today I'm grateful for: ________________

My Thoughts about the Day: ________________

Date: ________________

Today I'm grateful for: ________________

My Thoughts about the Day: ________________

Date: ________________

Today I'm grateful for: ________________

My Thoughts about the Day: ________________

Date: ________________

Today I'm grateful for: ____________________________________

My Thoughts about the Day: ______________________________

Date: ________________

Today I'm grateful for: ________________

My Thoughts about the Day: ________________

Date: ____________________

Today I'm grateful for: ____________________

My Thoughts about the Day: ____________________

Date: ________________

Today I'm grateful for: ____________________________________

My Thoughts about the Day: ______________________________

Date: ________________

Today I'm grateful for: ____________________________________

My Thoughts about the Day: ______________________________

Date: ______________

Today I'm grateful for: ______________

My Thoughts about the Day: ______________

Date: ____________

Today I'm grateful for: ____________

My Thoughts about the Day: ____________

Date: ______________

Today I'm grateful for: ______________

My Thoughts about the Day: ______________

Date: ________________

Today I'm grateful for: ______________________________

My Thoughts about the Day: __________________________

Date: ________________

Today I'm grateful for: ____________________

My Thoughts about the Day: ____________________

Date: ________________

Today I'm grateful for: ________________

My Thoughts about the Day: ________________

Date: ________________

Today I'm grateful for: ________________

My Thoughts about the Day: ________________

Date: ___________________

Today I'm grateful for: ___________________

My Thoughts about the Day: ___________________

Date: ________________

Today I'm grateful for: ____________________________________

My Thoughts about the Day: ______________________________

Date: ________________

Today I'm grateful for: ________________________________

My Thoughts about the Day: ________________________________

Date: ________________

Today I'm grateful for: ______________________________

My Thoughts about the Day: ______________________________

Date: ________________

Today I'm grateful for: ___________________________________

My Thoughts about the Day: ___________________________

Date: ________________

Today I'm grateful for: ____________________________________

My Thoughts about the Day: ______________________________

Date: ________________

Today I'm grateful for: ________________________________

My Thoughts about the Day: ________________________________

Date: ________________

Today I'm grateful for: ___________________________________

My Thoughts about the Day: ______________________________

Date: ________________

Today I'm grateful for: ____________________________________

My Thoughts about the Day: ______________________________

Date: ________________

Today I'm grateful for: ____________________________________

My Thoughts about the Day: ____________________________

Date: ________________

Today I'm grateful for: ________________

My Thoughts about the Day: ________________

Date: ________________

Today I'm grateful for: ________________________________

My Thoughts about the Day: ________________________________

Date: ____________

Today I'm grateful for: ____________

My Thoughts about the Day: ____________

Date: ________________

Today I'm grateful for: ________________________________

My Thoughts about the Day: ____________________________

Date: ________________

Today I'm grateful for: ____________________________________

My Thoughts about the Day: ______________________________

Date: ________________

Today I'm grateful for: ____________________________________

My Thoughts about the Day: ______________________________

Date: ________________

Today I'm grateful for: ____________________________________

My Thoughts about the Day: ________________________________

Date: ______________

Today I'm grateful for: ______________

My Thoughts about the Day: ______________

Date: ________________

Today I'm grateful for: ______________________________

My Thoughts about the Day: ______________________________

Date: ________________

Today I'm grateful for: ____________________________________

My Thoughts about the Day: ______________________________

Date: ________________

Today I'm grateful for: ____________________________________

My Thoughts about the Day: ______________________________

Date: ________________

Today I'm grateful for: ____________________________________

My Thoughts about the Day: ______________________________

Date: ________________

Today I'm grateful for: ____________________________________

My Thoughts about the Day: ______________________________

Date: ________________

Today I'm grateful for: ___________________________________

My Thoughts about the Day: ___________________________

Date: ________________

Today I'm grateful for: ______________________________

My Thoughts about the Day: __________________________

Date: ________________

Today I'm grateful for: ________________

My Thoughts about the Day: ________________

Date: ________________

Today I'm grateful for: ____________________________________

My Thoughts about the Day: ______________________________

Date: ______________

Today I'm grateful for: ______________________________

My Thoughts about the Day: ______________________________

Date: ________________

Today I'm grateful for: ____________________________________

My Thoughts about the Day: ____________________________

Date: ________________

Today I'm grateful for: ____________________________________

My Thoughts about the Day: ______________________________

Date: ________________

Today I'm grateful for: ________________

My Thoughts about the Day: ________________

Date: ________________

Today I'm grateful for: ____________________________________

My Thoughts about the Day: ______________________________

Date: ____________

Today I'm grateful for: ____________

My Thoughts about the Day: ____________

Date: ________________

Today I'm grateful for: ________________

My Thoughts about the Day: ________________

Date: ________________

Today I'm grateful for: ________________

My Thoughts about the Day: ________________

Date: ________________

Today I'm grateful for: ________________

My Thoughts about the Day: ________________

Date: ________________

Today I'm grateful for: ________________

My Thoughts about the Day: ________________

Date: ______________

Today I'm grateful for: ______________

My Thoughts about the Day: ______________

Date: ________________

Today I'm grateful for: ______________________________________

My Thoughts about the Day: ________________________________

Date: ________________

Today I'm grateful for: ____________________________________

My Thoughts about the Day: ______________________________

Date: ______________

Today I'm grateful for: ______________

My Thoughts about the Day: ______________

Date: ________________

Today I'm grateful for: ____________________________________

My Thoughts about the Day: ______________________________

Date: ________________

Today I'm grateful for: ____________________________________

My Thoughts about the Day: ________________________________

Date: ______________

Today I'm grateful for: ______________________________

My Thoughts about the Day: ______________________________

Date: ________________

Today I'm grateful for: ________________

My Thoughts about the Day: ________________

Date: ________________

Today I'm grateful for: ____________________________________

My Thoughts about the Day: ______________________________

Date: ________________

Today I'm grateful for: ____________________________________

My Thoughts about the Day: ______________________________

Date: ________________

Today I'm grateful for: ____________________________________

My Thoughts about the Day: ______________________________

Date: ________________

Today I'm grateful for: ________________________________

My Thoughts about the Day: ____________________________

Date: ______________

Today I'm grateful for: ______________________________

My Thoughts about the Day: ______________________________

Date: ________________

Today I'm grateful for: ____________________________________

My Thoughts about the Day: ________________________________

Date: ________________

Today I'm grateful for: ___________________________________

My Thoughts about the Day: ______________________________

Date: ________________

Today I'm grateful for: ________________

My Thoughts about the Day: ________________

Date: ________________

Today I'm grateful for: ________________

My Thoughts about the Day: ________________

Date: ______________

Today I'm grateful for: ______________

My Thoughts about the Day: ______________

Date: ________________

Today I'm grateful for: ________________

My Thoughts about the Day: ________________

Date: ______________

Today I'm grateful for: ______________________________

My Thoughts about the Day: ______________________________

Date: ________________

Today I'm grateful for: ___________________________________

My Thoughts about the Day: ______________________________

Date: ________________

Today I'm grateful for: ________________________________

My Thoughts about the Day: ________________________________

Date: ________________

Today I'm grateful for: ________________________________

My Thoughts about the Day: ____________________________

Date: ________________

Today I'm grateful for: ________________

My Thoughts about the Day: ________________

Date: ________________

Today I'm grateful for: ____________________________________

My Thoughts about the Day: ______________________________

Date: ________________

Today I'm grateful for: ____________________________________

My Thoughts about the Day: ______________________________

Date: ________________

Today I'm grateful for: ____________________________________

My Thoughts about the Day: ______________________________

Date: ________________

Today I'm grateful for: ____________________________________

My Thoughts about the Day: ______________________________

Date: ________________

Today I'm grateful for: ____________________________________

My Thoughts about the Day: ______________________________

Date: ________________

Today I'm grateful for: ____________________________________

My Thoughts about the Day: ______________________________

Date: ________________

Today I'm grateful for: ________________

My Thoughts about the Day: ________________

Date: ________________

Today I'm grateful for: ________________

My Thoughts about the Day: ________________

Date: ________________

Today I'm grateful for: ________________

My Thoughts about the Day: ________________

Date: ________________

Today I'm grateful for: ___________________________________

My Thoughts about the Day: ______________________________

Date: ________________

Today I'm grateful for: ________________________________

My Thoughts about the Day: ________________________________

Date: ________________

Today I'm grateful for: ____________________________________

My Thoughts about the Day: ______________________________

Date: ________________

Today I'm grateful for: ________________

My Thoughts about the Day: ________________

Date: ______________

Today I'm grateful for: ______________

My Thoughts about the Day: ______________

Date: ________________

Today I'm grateful for: ____________________________________

My Thoughts about the Day: ______________________________

Date: ________________

Today I'm grateful for: ________________

My Thoughts about the Day: ________________

Date: ________________

Today I'm grateful for: ________________________

My Thoughts about the Day: ________________________

Date: ________________

Today I'm grateful for: ________________

My Thoughts about the Day: ________________

Date: ________________

Today I'm grateful for: ________________________________

My Thoughts about the Day: ____________________________

Date: ________________

Today I'm grateful for: ________________________________

My Thoughts about the Day: __________________________

Date: ________________

Today I'm grateful for: ________________________________

My Thoughts about the Day: ____________________________

Date: ______________

Today I'm grateful for: ______________________________

My Thoughts about the Day: ______________________________

Date: ________________

Today I'm grateful for: ___________________________________

My Thoughts about the Day: ______________________________

Date: ______________

Today I'm grateful for: ______________________________

My Thoughts about the Day: ______________________________

Date: ________________

Today I'm grateful for: ________________________________

My Thoughts about the Day: ________________________________

Date: ________________

Today I'm grateful for: ________________

My Thoughts about the Day: ________________

Date: ________________

Today I'm grateful for: ______________________________

My Thoughts about the Day: __________________________

Date: ________________

Today I'm grateful for: ________________

My Thoughts about the Day: ________________

Date: ________________

Today I'm grateful for: ____________________________________

My Thoughts about the Day: ______________________________

Date: ________________

Today I'm grateful for: ____________________________________

My Thoughts about the Day: ______________________________

Date: ________________

Today I'm grateful for: ________________________________

My Thoughts about the Day: ________________________________

Date: ________________

Today I'm grateful for: ________________________________

My Thoughts about the Day: ______________________________

Date: ________________

Today I'm grateful for: ___________________________________

My Thoughts about the Day: ______________________________

Date: ________________

Today I'm grateful for: ____________________________________

My Thoughts about the Day: ______________________________

Date: ______________

Today I'm grateful for: ______________________________

My Thoughts about the Day: ______________________________

Date: ________________

Today I'm grateful for: ____________________________________

My Thoughts about the Day: ______________________________

Date: ________________

Today I'm grateful for: ______________________________________

My Thoughts about the Day: ______________________________

Date: ____________

Today I'm grateful for: ______________________________

My Thoughts about the Day: ______________________________

Date: ________________

Today I'm grateful for: ________________

My Thoughts about the Day: ________________

Date: ________________

Today I'm grateful for: ____________________________________

My Thoughts about the Day: ______________________________

Date: ________________

Today I'm grateful for: ____________________________________

My Thoughts about the Day: ______________________________

Date: ________________

Today I'm grateful for: ________________

My Thoughts about the Day: ________________

Date: ________________

Today I'm grateful for: ___________________________________

My Thoughts about the Day: ______________________________

Date: ______________

Today I'm grateful for: ______________________________

My Thoughts about the Day: ______________________________

Date: ________________

Today I'm grateful for: ____________________________________

My Thoughts about the Day: ______________________________

Date: ________________

Today I'm grateful for: ____________________________________

My Thoughts about the Day: ________________________________

Congratulations! You've now lived a year filled with gratitude!

VISIT MELISSA ALVAREZ ONLINE AT
www.MelissaA.com
www.APsychicHaven.com
Email Melissa at media@melissaa.com

www.ingramcontent.com/pod-product-compliance
Lightning Source LLC
Chambersburg PA
CBHW071259110426
42743CB00042B/1109
* 9 7 8 1 5 9 6 1 1 1 1 1 0 *